Real Estate Investor's Perspective

Somto Ubezonu, Ph.D.
Real Estate Investor

Real Estate Investor's Perspective

PENDIUM PUBLISHING HOUSE
514-201 DANIELS STREET
RALEIGH, NC 27605

For information, please visit our Web site at
www.pendiumpublishing.com

PENDIUM Publishing and its logo
are registered trademarks.

Real Estate Investor's Perspective
By Somto Ubezonu, Ph.D.

Copyright © Somto Ubezonu, Ph.D., 2013
All Rights Reserved.

ISBN: 978-1-936513-75-8

PUBLISHER'S NOTE

Without limiting the rights under the copyright reserved above, no part of this publication may be reproduced, stored in or introduced into a retrieval system, or transmitted, in any form, or by any means (electronic, mechanical, photocopying, recording, or otherwise), without the prior written permission of both the copyright owner and the above publisher of this book.

If you purchased this book without a cover you should be aware that the book is stolen property. It was reported as "unsold and destroyed" to the publisher and neither the author nor the publisher has received any payment for this "stripped book."

This book is printed on acid-free paper.

GRATITUDE

I am extending many thanks and gratitude to my wife, Ijeoma, and the children, Chukwuemeka and Chukwuma, for their constant support while writing this book.

DEDICATION

This book is dedicated to those who work hard to accomplish a desired goal and to those that have been oppressed in one way or the other.

I would also like to dedicate this book to my late brother, Dr. Chukwudifu Ubezonu (Barrister-at-law), who passed away at a very young age and to my daughter, Chinazom (Chy-Chy) Ubezonu, who also passed away at a very tender age. May they continue to rest in the bossom of our Lord Jesus Christ.

Acknowledgement

I am extremely delighted to give the Almighty God the honour and the admiration to work on this book. I am equally thanking God for giving me the strength, courage, and good health to work on this book. Let me extend special thanks to my parents, Justice Eugene Chukwuemeka and Mrs. Janet N. Ubaezonu, for their constant support and encouragement throughout the period of writing this book. I am equally thankful to my siblings: Ada, Ikenna, Chinedum, and Eziwanne for their support.

I am also thankful to Attorney Reginald Momah and Judge Dave N. Momah for getting me started in the United States and providing me with accommodations whenever school was out during my undergraduate days.

Finally I am equally thankful to those who have contributed in one way or the other to make this book a reality, especially to Dr. Arthrell Sanders for editing the script and to Dr. Fred Nwosu who wrote the foreword. Also special gratitude to Pastor Paul Adom and the prayer team of All Nations Restoration Fire Church (ANRFC) for their prayers. May we continue to remain blessed in Jesus' Name.

Author's Note

At the time of writing this book, I have been in the Real Estate business for slightly more than twelve years. I have made money and at the same time have lost money in the Real Estate business. I may not have made enough money to be a millionaire by the American standard; however, I have made a reasonable amount of money, enough to be able to send my children to a private Christian school, to take some good vacations, and to buy a few nice things for myself. I say "to God be the Glory."

I take full responsibility for everything written in this book. I have reflected on my experiences as a Real Estate Investor to the best of my ability. This book may not have been 100% perfect, but I believe that I have produced a book that provides a clear understanding for anybody to read and comprehend. Furthermore, this book is a combination of personal experiences as well as extensive research work.

The experiences acquired from the Real Estate business have enhanced my ability to negotiate in many business transactions in order to make a deal. Having the power to negotiate is awesome. Communicating well is very vital to negotiating well. Real Estate is a peoples' business. Regardless of what you do in real estate, you will be dealing with people.

Part of the proceeds from this book will go to S. Ubez Educational Foundation. The purpose of this foundation is to assist students in rural communities in Nigeria who come from less privileged families but would like to pursue a university education.

To make additional pledges, donations and order more copies of this book, please contact:

Dr. Somto Ubezonu
P.O. Box 51574
Durham, NC 27717
(919) 618-0218
080 569 81333
e-mail: ubezfoundations@yahoo.com

Words of Encouragement

- "If you are going to have a big goal, you need a strong mission to push you through the process. With a strong mission anything is attainable."
  Robert Kiyosaki, Entrepreneur

- "You have to believe in yourself when no one else does. That is what makes you a winner."
  Venus Williams, Olympic Gold Medalist & Professional Tennis Champion

- "Nothing happens in life until you take action."
  Dr. Somto Ubezonu, Real Estate Investor

- "Ninety-nine percent of all failures come from people who have a habit of making excuses."
  George W. Carver, Chemist

Table of Contents

Gratitude i
Dedication iii
Acknowledgement v
Author's Note vii
Words of Encouragement ix
Foreword xiii

Chapter 1: Getting into the Real Estate Business 1
Chapter 2: Buying Properties 8
Chapter 3: Selling Properties 19
Chapter 4: As a Seasoned RE Investor 27
Chapter 5: Having a Power Team 33
Chapter 6: How the Financial Crisis of 2008
              Affected the Real Estate Business 37
Chapter 7: Financing Real Estate Deals 42
Chapter 8: Doing Real Estate in a Foreign
              Country Especially Nigeria 46
Chapter 9: Faith in God and the Power of Prayer 50

Conclusion 57
References 59
Index 61
About the Author 63

Foreword

I am pleased to be asked by Dr. Somto Ubezonu to write the foreword for this book: Real Estate Investor's Perspective. since my first meeting with Dr. Somto Ubezonu (Ubez) I have not ceased to wonder how an individual could be so passionately involved in a business task. I soon discovered that the man possesses the characteristics of successful people. Tenacity is one of his traits. He pursues excellence in the delivery of tasks facing him.

The book, Real Estate Investor's Perspective, is a head-on attack on the subject of practical real estate business. The only way anyone can learn about practical business is through listening and gleaning from a practitioner of that business. Dr. Somto Ubez closed real estate deals in and out of the United states even while I did not know what he did for a living. I knew, however, that the man was up to something in whatsoever it was that he was doing. When I finally learned about his activities, I was not surprised.

Real Estate Investing coaches use terminology that can put off an interested mentee. This book that Dr. Somto Ubez has written contains a few of such known names. I have also read the works from those stables. However, I must state that the author of this book stripped the subject-matter of all the meandering details and delivered the knowledge in a pragmatic manner that is characteristic of himself.

Though it is not rare, Dr. Ubez did not hesitate to give credits to his creator, God, in this book. He did not mind letting the reader know his mental, psychological, socialogical, psychic, and locational locus. He has not claimed to be the best real estate coach, but any knowledge seeker within the real estate domain will not regret spending the little amount of time (compared to what the purported big real estate coaches might take) to learn from Dr. Somto Ubez how to flip property. His knowledge of the financial crisis reveals that he can lead the way through stormy real estate environments. His reference to the power of prayer is one of those rare tangents that one might ignore or avoid. My encounter with Dr. Somto Ubez, and especially the things that he said when I interviewed him for my television show, revealed that he is well positioned to either coach a real estate mentee or guide a new real estate investor. Why would anyone walk in the dark when Dr. Somto Ubez could well be the real estate investing light?

> Frederick Nwosu, Ph.D.
> Professor of Business Finance

CHAPTER 1

Getting into the Real Estate Business

After years of working for Corporate America and doing all sorts of jobs while in graduate school, and being laid off from a corporate job, I decided to get into the Real Estate (RE) business. I have also attended various seminars on RE to help prepare me for the RE business/investments.

I have always believed that through real estate, people may be able to increase their net-worth tremendously. Real Estate investments have always been a business that I wanted to get into because of helping to reach a financial goal faster. Real Estate business is a powerful tool for building and preserving wealth.

There are many benefits that go with Real Estate investing—from making deals where by the profit I can make is entirely up to me, building a life style some people only dream of. With the RE investing, I can own the business and work full or part time and be able to schedule my own time to be able to accomplish some other things.

The cash one can generate from the RE investments

may be unbelievable. During my extensive research on RE business and attending seminars, I found out that one can buy RE properties at a reasonable price, buy distressed properties, fix them up and rent them out or sell them after fix-up. Also one can generate income in RE with flipping properties.

Knowing the business and learning the skills is very helpful. I can always use the knowledge acquired to repeat the process many times on different properties, which will help increase profit without working too hard.

Real Estate is the kind of business whereby one has to build a power team to help increase and expedite your profit. It is a business where by people in your community, friends and family members can help you succeed. I know I can partner with other professionals like: RE lawyers, RE agents and brokers, mortgage brokers, home inspectors, contractors and mentors who can provide guidance during transactions.

I see the RE investments as a business full of opportunities. I can purchase distressed properties way below market value, fix them and sell to a potential buyer or another investor for a profit. In the process of improving or renovating the property, it can be flipped to another investor. In other words, the property does not have to be fully renovated before being flipped to another investor. The flipping is a quick way to sell a RE property and a longer way might be to rent the property out and have someone live there for a while before selling to the tenant or someone else.

Before getting into the RE business, I have always

looked at it as a business with many opportunities and very attractive. Take for instance in low income areas, one can find many opportunities for wholesaling or renovating properties. These opportunities can allow someone to provide clean and affordable housing to low income people while generating monthly rentals. Furthermore, in moderate income areas, I also believe that one can profit from excellent resale value and be able to work with a large market of first-time home buyers.

Knowing that property is in a prime location is another major reason of having the idea of getting into the RE business. A property at a prime location rises in value continuously, year after year. Before getting into the RE business, I have always heard RE investors say—location, location, location is the key to survival in the RE business. One can invest money in thousands of different businesses and lose them in a few months. However, if invested in a well lucrative area, it might be extremely hard to lose money just like that.

"A well-located RE is constantly increasing in value. There is almost nothing a sensible person can do that will permanently injure the value of well-located real estate." (Sheets, p.17) From all indications, it is impossible for anyone to go wrong in the RE business and not to make money as long as the property is in a lucrative area.

Working Fewer Hours

If one takes a look at different kinds of businesses—such as department stores, convenience stores, travel agencies— you may put in more than 8 hours a day. However, in the

RE business you can get by on a couple of hours a day. Why should I spend more than 40 hours a week on a business that I may not be able to make some money, whereas I can put in less than 20 hours a week and still make a reasonable amount of money in the RE business. I'm one of those that like to work short hours and still get the job done. RE is the kind of business you can do without putting in a lot of hours.

I have always had the mindset that the RE business will always give me the financial benefits other businesses may not be able to give me. RE will produce spendable cash flow that would be coming to me as a RE Investor on a weekly or monthly basis. The profits or returns coming from the RE investments can be used to improve living standards or to be re-invested in some other businesses. RE investments can sometimes give 100% return on investment.

In RE, one can control his investments unlike some other investments. "The success of your real estate investments may well rest on decisions that you make or fail to make." (Sheets, p.98) If one is a shareholder in an establishment, you may not be playing a major role in the pricing of a new product, but as a RE Investor you have the ultimate decision on whether to improve some of your properties or to do lease with the option of buying.

Having self-esteem and self-confidence is another reason for getting into the RE investments. The decision to be a Real Estate Investor has always been self-fulfilling.

Abraham Maslow, a human physiologist, studied people with healthy personalities and came to the conclusion that people have the ability to be creative in their decisions about life, and be determined to be whatever they want to be in life. (Sheets, p.116) Maslow further suggests that we must continue to move forward, one step at a time to achieve all of our God-given potential.

In the final analysis I have realized that the RE business is a business one cannot go wrong. It is very lucrative.

Dr. Somto Ubezonu at his Real Estate Office.

Dr. Somto Ubezonu making a presentation at a Real Estate business seminar.

CHAPTER 2

Buying Properties

Some of the points mentioned in this chapter are extracted from Part 2 of my first book: Experiences in Foreign Lands.

As a RE investor, when it comes to buying properties, one of the most important things to me is location and the neighborhood of the property to be purchased. Spending more money in a good area is more important to me than anything else. In looking at a particular location, I want to make sure that the neighborhood is safe, it is close to schools, banks, restaurants, churches, stores and business areas. I have to seriously believe in a location before deciding to invest in that area.

Most of the time when I am looking to invest on a property, I drive around town on some weekends or at my convenient time looking for investment properties to buy. When I am driving around town I am focused on locating "distressed properties." By distressed properties, I mean the properties that are in bad shape or completely run down, but in a good neighborhood. If the property is in a good neighborhood, once I have done the fix-up, the value of the property will go up. The reason why I focus more on these distressed properties is the kind of properties people are not interested in buying, however after repairs and fix-up they will look leavable. I am not worried how bad a piece of property looks as long as there is a good possibility of buying it and making the money once it is in a decent location.

As a matter of fact, distressed properties in good locations get me excited because there are opportunities to make money out of them. The money to be made is incredible. There are RE agents whom I have good rapport with sending me listings of different properties for sale. Also I take my time to drive to the properties to see how they look.

When I first got in the RE business, I never considered how important location was. However, with time and learning different things in the business, I came to realize the importance of location. From experience I realized that if I buy a property from a bad neighborhood, the chances of selling it fast is very slim.

Furthermore, buying RE properties include buying vacant lands. Since being in the RE business, I have been able to buy two vacant lands. The first one I bought, I was able to sell within two months. However, the second one I bought took me more than four years to sell. Although in a good location, however, the land was worthless because of some government restrictions. My initial plan of buying the land was to develop it and put up a structure. The sad experience I had was that the contractor that I hired to do some work for me embezzled a substantial amount of money that was paid to him and he ended up skipping town and was nowhere to be found. My advice to anyone purchasing a vacant land is to conduct a thorough research on the land to be able to find out what the land can be used for. You don't want to buy a vacant land and put up a structure and then realize you've made the worst mistake in your life when the structure may not be used for the purpose intended. That is why it's advisable to take the time to make sure all the dots are in order before making that decision.

Foreclosed properties are the kind of investment properties that I have invested in. Foreclosure is a situation whereby a homeowner is unable to continue to pay the mortgage and the bank or the lending institution will step in to sell the house at the auction. It is also a situation where a homeowner may not be able to pay the taxes on the property. When this happens then there is a legal process that follows.

James Banks, in his book, described two types of foreclosure: Judicial and Non-judicial. He described judicial foreclosure as when a "loan is in default . . . for the lender (mortgagor) to send a notice of intent to foreclose, sometimes called a Demand Letter to the borrower (mortgagee)." The purpose of this letter is to let the homeowner know that the loan is in default and the lender plans to take action if the owner does not bring the loan current.

Banks further identified that if the homeowner does not respond by a certain time to the Notice of Intent to foreclose, then the lender will file a legal action against the homeowner.

Banks also described a second type of foreclosure as a Non-judicial foreclosure. This is whereby foreclosure is used in "trust deed states or title theory states." When a borrower is in default, the lender instructs his lawyer to file a Notice of Default. A Notice of Default is the start of the foreclosure process. Period of redemption would normally follow the notice of default. (Banks, p.52)

Based on my readings and personal experiences, it is imperative to note the reasons why people go through foreclosure. In most cases a house owner can lose his home to foreclosure because of some unexpected situations beyond his control. These situations could be: divorce, job loss, illness, or medical expenses.

I have tried to purchase properties before they go to the auction, but have never been successful. Buying the property before the auction is simply trying to work out a deal with the seller in order to help salvage his credit. This works out for some investors. As for me, it has not.

As far as finding out when the property will be foreclosed, I can get detailed information from the tax office or court house depending on whether it's a tax or regular foreclosure. The auction is where the property is put up for, to the public for a sale. I have personally purchased a few properties at the auction and have been able to work out with great deals. Sometimes the auction is very competitive. I have seen investors purchase properties at a much higher amount than the property is worth.

It is very important to me to do a thorough research on any property that I plan to purchase at the auction and have an idea how high I would be bidding on the property. My advice to anyone purchasing property at the auction is to make sure that there is a clear title, no lien attached to the property and make sure whether the foreclosure is the 1st or 2nd mortgage that is being foreclosed on. Furthermore, I have always gone to see the property before the day of the auction, maybe a day or two before the auction day. This gives me an idea of the condition of the property and making possible provision for renovations and fix-ups. Whenever I get to the house, even if I cannot go inside the house because it's locked up, I try to peep in from the window just to have a good idea how things might be looking. I always keep in mind the worst situation knowing that sometimes some homeowners will end up vandalizing their property out of anger since they are going in for foreclosure, and they know that they would not be able to bring their mortgage current.

Once a foreclosure proceeding is finalized, there is a two-week redemption period. During this period the homeowner that lost the house to foreclosure will have about two weeks to redeem the house by paying up the balance owed on the mortgage.

In most cases, when I am ready to purchase investment properties, I will then ask some of the RE brokers that I work with to send me multiple listings which will show the available properties that are for sale. Those that are listed with RE agencies. When I receive the listings, I usually take my time to look at it thoroughly to be able to determine where the properties are located, how much they are priced for, whether there are properties for me in the listing and whether the right properties that I am interested in are in the good neighborhoods. As mentioned earlier, I am always looking for properties that are in a good neighborhood, even if they are distressed or need rehabilitation. All I have to do is look at the comparables, the properties that have been sold in these neighborhoods within the last year. Knowing the prices will determine whether the property I want to invest in is a good deal or not.

Once I make a decision on the properties that I am interested in buying, the next thing I have to decide on is whether I would like to purchase a property outright by paying cash immediately, which I have done in most cases, or whether I have to finance the property depending on my cash flow at the particular time. In RE business what can make or break a deal is financing. Putting your finances together for a deal is very important.

When all is set and done, when it comes to the purchase of a property, before making an offer, I have to do a thorough inspection on the property. A thorough inspection is the key to a successful RE investment. Normally, before making an offer, I will use a handyman to do the inspections. Sometimes I may use a licensed inspector, however I prefer to use a handyman because they are reasonable to work with and basically do the same thing a licensed inspector does. It varies on what the handyman can do or not do. Depending on the building, I may bring in an engineer to also look at the structure of the property.

Furthermore, when I am inspecting a property with my handyman, I am always willing to look beyond the obvious. Looking beyond the obvious may entail crawling in the crawl space of the structure to check for water damage, foundation damage, and plumbing problems. One thing I don't do is climbing on top of the roof of the building.

Also, during the inspection, I use an inspection check list (called Punch List or Property Inspection Report) which has detailed information on the exterior and interior of the building. The fix-ups from the report in the Punch List will determine the kind of offer to be made in order to purchase the property.

The final process I have to go through in purchasing a property is agreeing on an acceptable offer by the seller after making some negotiations. Once an offer to purchase is finalized, then the next thing is to draft a Sales Contract between myself as the buyer and the seller. (Copy of a Sales Contract is attached at the end of the chapter.) In the contract, everything is spelled out clearly. There is the purchase price of the property, the seller's and the buyer's names and what they are supposed to do, the conditions and terms of the contract including the date of the closing, and the venue for the closing. This is the day and the place the paperwork and ownership is transferred from the seller to me as the buyer.

It is important to note that for one to make money in the RE business, you have to make an offer. If offers are not made then one cannot finalize a deal. When I make offers on a property, I am not worried how low the offer may be. The most important thing for me is to make sure it's an offer I can live with.

Finally, when I am getting ready to make an offer on a property, I always ask the question, why does a potential seller want to sell? Is the seller desperate to sell? All these questions are extremely important to me before making an offer and probably before making the last offer.

Somto Ubezonu discussing with one of his contractors

Dr. Somto Ubezonu inspecting a property with his handy-man before purchasing.

BUYER'S PROPERTY INSPECTION REPORT

Property Address: _____

Noted below are my/our findings of the physical condition of the above mentioned real property as of _____ (mo./day) _____(yr.). Items not marked as UNSATISFACTORY are considered to be in satisfactory condition.

GENERAL BUILDING EXTERIOR	UNSATISFACTORY	ESTIMATED COST OF REPAIR, REPLACEMENT, OR ADDITION

Grounds
- Landscaping
- Pool
- Sewers or Septic Tank
- Sprinklers
- Other

Building
- Roof
- Chimney
- Foundation
- Wood Exteriors
- Other

GENERAL BUILDING INTERIOR

Heating And Air Conditioning Systems
- Furnace
- Air Conditioning
- Water Heater
- Other

Built-In Appliances And Equipment
- Ovens
- Burners
- Microwave
- Dishwasher
- Disposal
- Smoke Detectors
- Intercom
- Electric Garage Door Opener
- Other

Electrical Systems
- Interior Lighting
- Exterior Lighting
- Other

Plumbing
- Bathrooms
- Kitchen
- Laundry
- Other

Glass
- Windows
- Screens
- Window Panes
- Glass Doors
- Shower Glass
- Tub Enclosures
- Mirrors
- Other

Personal Property
- Carpets
- Draperies
- Other

TOTAL

REMARKS: _____

DATE: _____ PURCHASER: _____

REAL ESTATE SALES CONTRACT

WHEN COMPLETED AND SIGNED BY BOTH PARTIES, THIS IS A LEGALLY BINDING CONTRACT. IF THIS CONTRACT IS NOT FULLY UNDERSTOOD, THE SERVICES OF A COMPETENT PROFESSIONAL SHOULD BE SOUGHT.

Seller _____, hereby agrees to sell to Buyer, _____, or Buyer's nominee, the real property set forth below and all improvements thereon (herein referred to as the Property), and Buyer agrees to purchase said Property from the Seller on the terms and conditions set forth in this contract.

DESCRIPTION: The Property is located in _____ County, (city/state) _____ and is commonly known as (address) _____ has approximate lot dimensions of _____ x _____, and is legally described as follows:
(If the legal description is not included at the time of execution, it may be attached to and incorporated herein afterward.)

1. **PURCHASE PRICE:** The total purchase price to be paid for the Property by the Buyer is payable as follows:

(a) Initial deposit .... $ _____

(b) Sum due within _____ days after acceptance of this Contract .... $ _____

(c) Additional sum due at closing (not including prorations) .... $ _____

(d) Proceeds of new note and mortgage to be given by Buyer or any lender other than the Seller ... $ _____

(e) Existing mortgage on the Property which shall remain on the Property but which shall not subject Buyer to any penalty or fee or increase in the original interest rate of said mortgage ... $ _____

(f) Balance due Seller by promissory note of the Buyer subject to the requirements set forth in this contract ... $ _____

(g) Balance due Seller by Articles of Agreement for warranty deed .... $ _____

TOTAL PURCHASE PRICE .... $ _____

2. **APPORTIONMENT OF PURCHASE PRICE AND DEED:** Land $_____ Building $_____ Personal Property $_____ It is agreed that the Property will be conveyed by recordable _____ warranty deed, with release of dower and homestead rights, subject to general real estate taxes for the current year, covenants, conditions, restrictions of record, and easements of record, all of which must be acceptable to Buyer.

3. Buyer will pay for recordation of deed and prorated share of prepaid insurance, taxes, and interest, if any.

4. The Seller will pay for: [ ] Revenue stamps (State, county, and local); [ ] Title commitment in the amount of the purchase price from _____ or any title insurance company duly licensed to underwrite title insurance in the state of _____; [ ] Survey; [ ] _____ Attorney's fees; [ ] Appraisal fee; [ ] Real estate commission; [ ] Title abstract; [ ] Title opinion letter; [ ] F.H.A./ V.A. mortgage discount; [ ] Photographs; [ ] Satisfaction of mortgage and recording fee; [ ] Lead paint inspection; [ ] Home inspection; [ ] Repairs or replacements required by the F.H.A or V.A. not to exceed $_____; [ ] Any other inspections required by law. [ ] _____

5. **PRORATED ITEMS:** All rents, water taxes or charges, taxes, assessments, monthly mortgage insurance premiums, fuel, prepaid service contracts, and interest on existing mortgages shall be prorated as of the date of closing. If Buyer is to accept the Property, subject to an existing mortgage requiring an escrow deposit for taxes, insurance, and/or other items, all escrow payments required to be made up to the time of closing shall be made to the escrow holder at Seller's expense and said escrow balance shall be assigned to the Buyer without compensation to the Seller; it being expressly understood that said escrow balance is included in the Total Purchase Price. All mortgage payments required of Seller to be made shall be current as of the time of closing. If the exact amount of real estate taxes cannot be ascertained at the time of closing, Seller agrees to prorate said taxes on the basis of 110% of the last ascertainable amount.

6. **TITLE AND TITLE INSURANCE:** Within _____ days [ ] after the date of acceptance of this contract [ ] after the date of approval of Buyer's mortgage loan (if any), the Seller will provide and deliver to Buyer or Buyer's Attorney: [ ] A title commitment for an owner's title insurance policy in the amount of the purchase price (to be issued by a title insurance company duly licensed by the state of _____, to underwrite title insurance); [ ] A title insurance commitment for a mortgage policy in the amount of $_____. [ ] A continuation of abstract.

7. **SURVEY:** Within _____ days [ ] after the date of acceptance of this contract [ ] after the date of approval of Buyer's mortgage loan (if any), the Seller will provide and deliver to Buyer or Buyer's Attorney: [ ] A new spotted certified survey having all corners staked and showing all improvements upon the Property. [ ] No survey is required.

8. **EXAMINATION OF TITLE AND TIME OF CLOSING:** If the title evidence and survey as specified above disclose that Seller is vested with fee simple title to the Property (subject only to the permitted exceptions set forth above acceptable to Buyer), this sale shall be closed and Buyer shall perform the agreements made in this contract, at the office of Buyer's Attorney, on or before [ ] _____ [ ] _____ days after the mortgage loan approval [ ] _____ days after acceptance of this contract. If title evidence or survey reveal any defect or condition which is not acceptable to Buyer, the Buyer shall, within fifteen (15) days, notify the Seller of such title defects and Seller agrees to use reasonable efforts to remedy such defects and shall have thirty (30) days to do so, in which case this sale shall be closed within ten (10) days after delivery of acceptable evidence to Buyer and Buyer's Attorney that such defects have been cured. Seller agrees to pay for and clear all delinquent taxes, liens, and other encumbrances, unless the parties otherwise agree. If Seller is unable to convey to Buyer a good and insurable title to the Property, the Buyer shall have the right to demand all sums deposited by Buyer and held by or for the Seller. At the same time, Buyer shall return to Seller all items, if any, received from Seller, whereupon all rights and liabilities of the parties to this contract shall cease. However, the Buyer shall have the right to accept such title as Seller may be able to convey and to close this sale upon the other terms as set forth in this contract.

9. **DEFAULT BY BUYER:** If Buyer fails to perform the agreements of this contract within the time set forth herein, Seller may retain, as liquidated damages and not as a penalty, all of the initial deposit specified in paragraph 1(a) above, it being agreed that this is Seller's exclusive remedy.

10. **DEFAULT BY SELLER:** If Seller fails to perform any of the agreements of this contract, all deposits made by Buyer shall be returned to Buyer on demand, or the buyer may bring suit against Seller for damages resulting from the breach of contract, or the Buyer may bring an action for specific performance. Buyer's remedies are cumulative and not exclusive of one another, and all other remedies shall be available in either law or equity to Buyer for Seller's breach hereof.

11. **CONDOMINIUM PROVISION:** (a) If the subject property is a condominium unit, this contract is subject to the condition that Seller be able to obtain release or waiver of any right of first refusal or other preemptive rights of purchase created by the Declaration of Condominium within the time established by said Declaration. If, after making every reasonable effort, Seller is unable to obtain such release or waiver within the time provided and so notifies Buyer within that time, this contract shall become null and void and all of Buyer's deposits shall be returned to the Buyer, provided that if said option or preemptive right is not exercised within the time specified by the Declaration of Condominium, this contract shall remain in full force and effect for that period of time which the Declaration of Condominium provides for completion of the sale, should the option or preemptive right not be exercised. If the Declaration of Condominium contains no such option or preemptive right, this paragraph shall be null and void and not part of this contract. (b) Seller represents and warrants that there are no condominium assessments currently due and owing. Seller agrees to pay any assessments, including special assessments, that have been or will be levied at any time prior to the date of closing.

12. **ATTORNEY FEES AND COSTS:** If any litigation is instituted with respect to enforcement of the terms of this contract, the prevailing party shall be entitled to recover all costs incurred, including, but not limited to, reasonable attorney's fees and court costs.

13. **RISK OF LOSS OR DAMAGE:** Risk of loss or damage to the Property by any cause is retained by the seller until closing.

14. **CONDITION OF THE PROPERTY:** Seller agrees to deliver the Property to Buyer in its present condition, ordinary wear and tear excepted, and further certifies and represents that seller knows of no latent defect in the Property. All heating, cooling, plumbing, electrical, sanitary systems, and appliances shall be in good working order at the time of closing. Seller represents and warrants that the personal property conveyed with the premises shall be the same property inspected by Buyer and that no substitutions will be made without the Buyer's written consent. Buyer may also inspect or cause to be inspected the foundation, roof supports, or structural member of all improvements located upon the Property. If any such system, appliance, roof, foundation, or structural member shall be found defective, Buyer shall notify Seller at or before closing and Seller shall thereupon remedy the defect forthwith at his/her sole expense (in which case the time for closing shall be reasonably extended as necessary). If the costs of such repairs shall exceed 5% of the total purchase price, Seller may elect not to make such repairs and the Buyer may elect to take the Property in such defective condition and deduct 5% from the purchase price or Buyer may, at his/her option, elect to terminate this contract and receive the full refund of all deposits and other sums tendered hereunder. In addition, seller agrees to remove all debris from the Property by date of possession.

15. **OCCUPANCY:** Seller shall deliver possession to Buyer no later than the closing date unless otherwise stated herein. Seller represents that there are no persons occupying the Property except the following tenants of the Seller: _____

Seller agrees to deliver exclusive occupancy of the Property to Buyer at the time of closing unless otherwise specifically stated herein. Seller agrees to provide true and accurate copies of all written leases to Buyer within five (5) days after the date of acceptance of this contract. Said leases are subject to Buyer's approval. Seller shall provide such letters notifying tenants to pay rent to the buyer after closing as Buyer may reasonably request. Seller warrants that any rent rolls and other income and expense data provided to Buyer are complete and accurate, all of which must be acceptable to Buyer.

16. [ ] MORTGAGE OR THIRD PARTY FINANCING: According to paragraph 1(d) of this contract, it is agreed that Buyer will require a new mortgage loan to finance this purchase. The application for this mortgage will be made with a lender acceptable to Buyer, and unless a mortgage loan, acceptable to Buyer, is approved without contingencies other than those specified in this contract within _____ days from the date of acceptance of this contract, the Seller or Buyer shall have the right to terminate this contract and, at that time, all sums deposited by Buyer shall be returned to Buyer and Buyer shall return any surveys and copies of leases received from Seller. Notwithstanding the aforesaid provisions, if Buyer so requests and if Seller agrees, Seller shall have _____ days to offer Buyer a purchase money mortgage on said property at terms acceptable to and approved by buyer, and this contract shall remain in full force and effect. Said purchase money mortgage shall be fully subject to the terms and conditions of the paragraph relating to Seller Financing below.

17. [ ] SELLER FINANCING: According to paragraph 1(f) above, it is understood that the Buyer will execute and deliver at the closing, a Promissory Note to Seller which shall provide for full or partial prepayment without penalty [ ] and shall bear interest at the rate of _____% per annum beginning on _____ in the amount of $_____ per _____ [ ] such that the amount of such payments shall amortize the debt due in _____ years with all unpaid principal and interest due _____. The said Promissory Note shall be secured by a mortgage acceptable to Buyer and providing for the full and free right of the mortgagor to transfer the Property, in whole or in part, subject to the mortgage and to substitute for the Property other collateral of equivalent equity value; the exculpation of the mortgagor from personal liability; thirty (30) days prior written notice to the mortgagor of the mortgagee's intention to commence foreclosure proceedings and the right of the mortgagor to cure; the subordination of mortgagee's lien to an existing or future senior encumbrance; the right of first refusal in the mortgagor if the mortgagee shall at any time sell its interest at a discount; future advances at the option of the mortgagee; the release or portions of the Property from the lien of the mortgage upon partial principal payments by mortgagor, which said portion shall be released in the same proportion that the amount of the partial payment bears to the then outstanding principal balance.

18. [ ] ARTICLES OF AGREEMENT FOR WARRANTY DEED: If this sale is made by Articles of Agreement for warranty deed pursuant to paragraph 1(g) above, then the terms of paragraph 17 relating to Seller Financing shall be incorporated in said Articles of Agreement and shall become a part thereof, and the terms relating to a Promissory Note and mortgage shall be construed and relate to the Articles of Agreement for warranty deed in lieu of any reference to Promissory Note and mortgage.

19. F.H.A. FINANCING: It is expressly agreed that, notwithstanding any other provisions of this contract, Buyer shall not be obligated to complete the purchase of the Property described herein or to incur any penalty by forfeiture of any money deposit or otherwise unless the Seller has delivered to the Buyer a written statement issued by the Federal Housing Commissioner setting forth the appraised value of the Property (excluding closing costs) of not less than $_____ which statement Seller agrees to deliver to the Buyer promptly after such appraised value statement is made available to Seller. The Buyer shall, however, have the privilege and option of proceeding with the consummation of this contract without regard to the amount of the appraised valuation made by the Federal Housing Commissioner.

20. V.A. FINANCING: It is expressly agreed that, notwithstanding any other provisions of this contract, the Buyer shall not incur any penalty by forfeiture of earnest money or otherwise be obligated to complete the purchase of the Property described in this contract if the Total Purchase Price exceeds the reasonable value of the Property established by the Veterans Administration. The buyer shall, however, have the privilege and option of completing this transaction without regard to the amount of reasonable value established by the Veterans Administration.

21. [ ] TERMITE INSPECTION: Seller agrees to furnish to Buyer, at Seller's expense, an inspection report showing all buildings on the Property to be free and clear from visible infestation and free from visible dry or wet rot damage by termites and other wood-destroying organisms. This inspection report is to be furnished by a licensed pest control firm. If a report shows such visible infestation or damage, Seller shall pay all costs of treatment of such infestation and all costs of repair of such damage. If the costs of treatment and repair shall exceed 3% of the total sale price, Seller may elect not to make such treatment and repairs and Buyer may elect to take the Property in its then condition and deduct 3% from the total purchase price and complete the transaction or Buyer may terminate this contract and receive a full refund of all deposits made by Buyer hereunder.

22. [ ] ZONING: Unless the property is properly zoned for _____ use and there are no deed restrictions against such use at the time of closing, the Buyer shall have the right to terminate this contract and receive a full refund of all deposits made by Buyer hereunder.

23. LEGAL USE: Seller represents and warrants to Buyer that the entire property conforms to all building codes and restrictions that may be imposed by any governmental agency either national, state, or local. Seller also warrants that there are no building code violations on the Property and that Seller has received no notice of any building code violations for the past ten years that have not been fully corrected.

24. LOCAL ORDINANCES: Seller shall procure for Buyer, at Seller's expense, all certificates of inspection, certificates of occupancy, or the like required under the terms of any local ordinance.

25. PERSONAL PROPERTY INCLUDED IN THE PURCHASE PRICE: (Strike items not applicable): storm and screen doors and windows; awnings; outdoor television antenna; wall-to-wall, hallway, and stair carpeting; window shades and draperies and supporting fixtures; venetian blinds; electric plumbing and other fixtures as installed; water softener; attached shelving; hardware; trees and shrubs; refrigerator(s) _____; stove(s) _____; air conditioner(s) _____ and such other items as is listed below or on a rider attached hereto, all of which personal property is unencumbered and owned by Seller. All such items shall be conveyed from Seller to Buyer by a Bill Of Sale.

26. [ ] This offer shall terminate if not accepted before *(mo./day)* _____, *(yr.)* _____

27. R.E.S.P.A. COMPLIANCE: Seller and Buyer agree to make all disclosures and do all things necessary to comply with the provisions of the Real Estate Settlement Procedures Act of 1974 if it is applicable to this transaction.

28. ADDITIONAL TERMS AND CONDITIONS:

(a) Where the context requires, the terms that Seller and Buyer shall include are in the masculine as well as the feminine and the singular as well as the plural.

(b) There are no agreements, promises, or understandings between the parties except as specifically set forth in this contract. No alterations or changes shall be made to this contract unless the same are in writing and signed or initialed by the parties hereto.

(c) The provisions of this contract shall survive the closing and shall not merge in any deed of conveyance herein.

(d) This agreement shall be construed under the laws of the State of _____.

(e) Other:

29. REAL ESTATE SALES COMMISSION: The Seller agrees to pay all real estate sales commission due on this transaction.

30. NOTICES: Any notices required to be given herein shall be sent to the parties listed below at their respective addresses either by personal delivery or by certified mail - return receipt requested. Such notice shall be effective upon delivery or mailing.

TIME IS OF THE ESSENCE OF THIS AGREEMENT.

In witness whereof, the parties signed their names on the dates in the year set forth below.

Buyer(s): _____

_____

_____

Buyer's Date of Offer *(mo./day)* _____ *(yr.)* _____

Address: _____

Address: _____

Seller(s): _____

_____

_____

Seller's Date of Acceptance: *(mo./day)* _____ *(yr.)* _____

Address: _____

Address: _____

© The Professional Education Institute

CHAPTER 3

Selling Properties

As a RE investor, one of the things I do is to sell properties. As mentioned in Chapter 1, flipping a property is one of the ways of selling property to another investor or to a potential buyer for a quick profit.

Whenever I have a property for sale and if there are no serious activities going on or with no offers coming in, then I have the option of revisiting the price. The RE business is unpredictable that prices can fluctuate depending on what is going on at a particular time. Whenever it comes to pricing a property, I consider the comparables and the kind of fix-ups that has to be done on the property. Sometimes, once I know that a property that I would like to sell is in a good location and very valuable, I try not to worry as much, realizing that it's just a matter of time before it will be sold.

I have done lease options with some properties. Lease option is a process of having tenants live in the property for about two years before selling the property to the tenant. The tenant can choose to do sweat equity, whereby all the expenses he has made on the property can go towards the down payment for the property. This option is equally good for potential buyers who may need time to repair their credit history. (Form for Lease Option is attached at the end of the chapter).

As a RE investor, I purchase properties, renovate, and turn around and sell immediately. Sometimes I may want to rent it out for a while and then sell. Regardless of whether I would like to sell immediately or hold it for some time, at the end of the day is to sell and make a substantial profit once the property is sold.

Working with Real Estate Agents or Brokers

I do have RE agents and brokers that I work with most of the time. I always make sure that they understand how much that I have invested in a particular property and how valuable the property may be to me. However, I don't feel bad if I am advised that the property may be worth less than what is expected.

I have the agent advertise the property for sale in the Multiple Listing Service (MLS). It is the responsibility of the agent to pre-qualify potential buyers, screen applicants and negotiate the sale on my behalf. I have also sold my properties without the help of an agent. I do have agents handy to help out with the sale unless I have some other things I am working on. When I am selling my property by myself, I usually display For Sale by Owner (FSBO). If I am using an agent, then he will display his company sign.

One can attract more buyers to a property by putting up a road sign. However, these buyers will not be of the same quality as those who may find you through a more targeted advertising. Roadside signs and signs placed in front of the house may attract people who live nearby or people who have a reason to be in your neighborhood for various reasons.

Choosing the right agent is very important. One who is dedicated, honest and hard-working is something that takes time to find. I have always taken my time to find out good agents to be able to work with. Once in a while, I do run into bad ones but generally have worked with good ones. A good agent will always listen and address my concerns. A good agent realizes that once I am happy at the end of any transaction, then he will also be happy. The best agent for me is the one that has my best interest at heart. I also try to treat them well because they generate good leads for me.

As far as selling any of my properties, I have to familiarize myself with the legal forms, pricing market and the disclosure laws so that if I am advertising a property I have to make sure it is done properly to avoid being sued by a buyer because I failed to disclose one thing or the other. Pointing out the problems in a disclosure form is very important to avoid unnecessary headaches. It is always good to do this disclosure properly to the best of your knowledge.

Bill Effros in his book: <u>How to Sell Your Home in Five Days</u>: advised that when you are trying to sell your home, what you are really trying to do is to find the buyer who is willing to pay the most money. (Effros, p.7) When I have a property for sale, of course, I am always looking for the buyer that would pay the most. Sometimes it might depend on how desperate I am at a particular time to sell. In most cases, if I don't have a serious buyer and someone comes up with an amount that is reasonable then I will end up selling the property. There have been situations that I was bent on getting the most money for a property and the property may end up being on the market for a long time until the price is significantly reduced. Sometimes the sale price may have to be reduced about three or four times before it is finally sold.

Effros, in his book further advised the method of selling a property within a five-day period. Per his advice, if you start on a day like Wednesday:

Day 1 – Wednesday: Run an ad offering your home for 50% of what you think it's worth or best offer. Allow the ad to continue to run until Sunday.

Days 2 and 3 – Thursday and Friday: If you don't get up to 23 responses by Friday night, you've set your price too high. (Think about reducing the sale or starting all over again.)

Day 4 – Saturday: Show the property and allow buyers to leave bids.

Day 5 – Sunday: Continue to show your home until 5pm. Starting at 8pm, start calling buyers who left bids to determine who will pay the most for the property.

Day 6 – Monday: Contact the RE agent who will help you close on the home in a manner typical of the area in which you live. (Effros, p.22)

Bill Effros analysis of selling your home in a five-day period is very interesting and how I wish that his analysis would always work for me whenever I have an investment property for sale. The shortest period that I have had an investment property on the market is two weeks.

Whenever I have an investment property for sale, I always make enough room for any potential buyer to make some negotiations. Even when I am buying, I do some serious negotiations depending on the location and the value of the property. It's very imperative for both sides to understand the importance of negotiations. Properties in the same neighborhood that are even identically built at the same time may not be priced the same because of the things like the upgrades, maintenance, or whether a particular property is on a cul-de-sac or not.

Another way of putting an investment property up for sale is by having a data base. In the data base, there is a list of names of individuals that are always looking for properties to buy, either for investment purposes or to live in there. Anytime I have a property available for sale, I have to look in the data base to find out who might be interested in purchasing a property, depending on the price. The names in the data base always have price range attached to it. Because of the fact that the names in the data base continue to change on a regular basis with people entering and exiting in it, my job is to keep it current.

There have been situations whereby I have potential buyers that want to pay cash out right. If a buyer wants to pay cash, I don't really need to pre-qualify the person. All I need is a letter from the bank verifying that the funds are there to close the deal. Cash deals are always fast and the closing can be done as soon as possible. With financing or trying to borrow the funds from the bank may take a longer time. Also with a buyer who wants to finance then I have to pre-qualify to make sure he or she can afford to buy the property. One of the reasons for pre-qualifying is to save myself some time from potential buyers who are not serious. Pre-qualification entails looking into the credit history, the buyer's income, expenses every month, etc.

In the final analysis, placing an ad in the paper has been a very important way of selling my investment properties. I have always placed my ads where they can be seen by potential buyers. I advertise in the local newspapers as well as on Craig's List.

When placing an ad, I always keep in mind to put a price people are willing to pay. I try to make the ad look attractive to give the buyers encouragement to attend the Open House or at least call with some serious questions. Furthermore, when I am writing the ad, I try to make it very clear in order to get the information across properly.

Effros further advised in his book that people prepare themselves before attempting to place a classified ad in a newspaper. He further advised that you have to take the time to make sure it's right.

If I am selling the property myself without advertising with a RE agent, usually my ad would say: House for Rent or Sale by Owner. Three bedrooms with two full baths. Average-sized living room. Asking price is $79,900 or best offer. Call . . . and would have an Open House on . . . . I don't really give out detailed information when I am placing an ad in the paper.

RESIDENTIAL LEASE WITH OPTION TO PURCHASE

THIS AGREEMENT made and entered into on this _____ day of (mo.) _____ (yr.) _____ by and between _____
hereinafter called Lessor and _____ and/or assigns, hereinafter called Lessee: The Lessor, for and in consideration of
the sum of _____ dollars in hand paid by the Lessee, receipt of which is hereby acknowledged, hereby leases to Lessee, his/her heirs or
assignees, the premises situated in the City of _____ County of _____ State of _____ legally described
as _____
_____

(If the legal description is not included at the time of execution, it may be attached to and incorporated herein afterward.)
(Street Address: _____) and consisting of _____ upon the following
TERMS and CONDITIONS:

1. Personal Property: Said lease shall include the following personal property: _____
_____

2. Term: The term hereof shall commence on (mo./day) _____, (yr.) _____, and continue for a period of _____ months thereafter.

3. Rent: Rent shall be $_____ per month, payable in advance, upon the first day of each calendar month to Lessor or his/her authorized
agent at the following address: _____
or at such other places as may be designated by Lessor from time to time. In the event rent is not paid within five (5) days after due date, Lessee agrees to
pay a late charge of $_____ plus interest at _____ % per annum on the delinquent amount.

4. Utilities: Lessee shall be responsible for the payment of all utilities and services except _____
which shall be paid by the Lessor.

5. Use: The premises shall be used as a residence and for no other purpose without prior written consent of Lessor.

6. House Rules: In the event that the premises are in a building containing more than one unit, Lessee agrees to abide by any and all house rules, whether promulgated before or after the execution hereof, including, but not limited to, rules with respect to noise, odors, disposal of refuse, pets, parking, and use of common areas.

7. Assignment And Subletting: Lessee may assign this agreement or sublet any portion of the premises without prior written consent of the Lessor.

8. Maintenance, Repairs, Or Alterations: Lessee shall maintain the premises in a clean and sanitary manner including all equipment, appliances, furniture and furnishings therein, and shall surrender the same at termination thereof, in as good condition as received, normal wear and tear excepted. Lessee shall be responsible for damages caused by his/her negligence and that of his/her family, or invitees or guests. Lessee shall maintain any surrounding grounds, including lawns and shrubbery, and keep the same clear of rubbish and weeds, if such grounds are part of the premises and are exclusively for use of the Lessee.

9. Entry and Inspection: Lessee shall permit Lessor or Lessor's agents to enter the premises at reasonable times and upon reasonable notice for the purpose of inspecting the premises or for making necessary repairs.

10. Possession: If Lessor is unable to deliver possession of the premises at the commencement hereof, Lessor shall not be liable for any damage caused thereby nor shall this agreement be void or voidable, but Lessee shall not be liable for any rent until possession is delivered. Lessee may terminate this agreement if possession is not delivered within _____ days of the commencement of the term hereof.

11. Security/Option Consideration: The security deposit of $_____ shall secure the performance of the Lessee's obligations hereunder. Lessor may, but shall not be obligated to, apply all or portions of said deposit on account of Lessee's obligations hereunder. Any balance remaining upon termination shall be returned to Lessee.

12. Deposit Funds: Any returnable deposits shall be refunded within fifteen (15) days from the date possession is delivered to Lessor or his/her authorized agent.

13. Attorney Fees: The prevailing party shall be entitled to all costs incurred in connection with any legal action brought by either party to enforce the terms hereof or relating to the demised premises, including reasonable attorneys' fees.

14. Notices: Any notice which either party may or is required to give may be given by mailing the same, postage prepaid, to Lessee or at such other places as may be designated by the parties from time to time.

15. Heirs, Assigns, Successors: This lease and option shall include and insure to and bind the heirs, executors, administrators, successors, and assigns of the respective parties hereto.

16. Time: Time is of the essence of this agreement. This offer shall terminate if not accepted before (mo./day) _____ (yr.) _____.

17. Holding Over: Any holding over after expiration of the term of this lease, with the consent of the Lessor, shall be construed as a month-to-month tenancy in accordance with the terms hereof, as applicable.

18. Default: If Lessee shall fail to pay rent when due or perform any term hereof after not less than three (3) days written notice of such default given in the manner required by law, the Lessor at his/her option may terminate all rights of the Lessee hereunder, unless Lessee, within said time, shall cure such default. If Lessee abandons or vacates the property while in default of payment of rent, Lessor may consider any property left on premises to be abandoned and may dispose of the same in any manner allowed by law. In the event the lessor reasonably believes that such abandoned property has no value, it may be discarded.

19. Option: Lessee shall have the option to purchase the leased premises described herein upon the following TERMS and CONDITIONS:
 a. The total purchase price shall be $_____ (_____ dollars)
 b. The purchase price shall be paid as follows:

20. Encumbrances: Lessee shall take title to the property subject to: 1) Real Estate Taxes not yet due and 2) Covenants, conditions, restrictions, reservations, rights, rights of way, and easements of record, if any.

21. Examination of Title: Lessee shall have fifteen (15) days from the date of receipt of title report to examine the title to the property and to report, in writing, any valid objections thereto. Any exceptions to the title which would be disclosed by examination of the records shall be deemed to have been accepted unless reported in writing within said fifteen (15) days. If Lessee objects to any exceptions to the title, Lessor shall use all due diligence to remove such exceptions at his/her own expense within sixty (60) days thereafter. But if such exceptions cannot be removed within the sixty (60) days allowed, all rights and obligations hereunder may, at the election of the Lessee, terminate and end unless he/she elects to purchase the property subject to such exceptions.

22. Evidence Of Title: Lessor shall provide evidence of Title in the form of a policy of title insurance at Lessor's expense.

23. Bill Of Sale: The personal property identified in paragraph _____ shall be conveyed by bill of sale.

24. Closing: Closing shall be within _____ days from exercise of the option unless otherwise extended by other terms of this agreement.

25. Prorations: Tax and insurance escrow account, if any, to be transferred intact to Lessee with no prorations. Interest and other expenses of the property to be prorated as of the date of closing. Unpaid real estate taxes, security deposits, advance rentals, or considerations involving future lease credits shall be credited to the Lessee.

26. Expiration Of Option: This option may be exercised at any time prior to its expiration at midnight (mo./day) _____ (yr.) _____. Upon expiration, Lessor shall be released from all obligations hereunder and all of Lessee's rights hereunder, legal or equitable, shall cease.

27. Exercise Of Option: The option shall be exercised by mailing or delivering written notice to the Lessor prior to the expiration of this option. Notice, if mailed, shall be by certified mail, postage prepaid, to the Lessor at the address set forth below, and shall be deemed to have been given upon the day shown on the postmark of the envelope in which such notice is mailed. In the event the option is exercised, _____ percent of the rent paid hereunder, as well as any security deposit paid, prior to the exercise of the option shall be credited upon the purchase price.

28. Right To Sell: Lessor warrants to Lessee that Lessor is the legal owner of the leased premises and has the legal right to sell leased premises under the terms and conditions of this agreement.

IN WITNESS WHEREOF, the parties hereto have executed this agreement the day and year first above written.

| _____ | _____ |
| LESSEE | LESSOR |

| _____ | _____ |
| LESSEE | LESSOR |

| _____ | _____ |
| ADDRESS | ADDRESS |

CHAPTER 4

As a Seasoned RE Investor

As of the time I am writing this book, I have been in the RE business for a little bit over 12 years, and I consider myself a seasoned RE investor. Throughout the 12-year plus period, I have made money and have also lost money on various RE deals. When a significant amount of money is made on a deal, it feels good, and when money is lost or did not make enough, it would look as if the entire world has turned upside down. As a seasoned investor, I have learned from different experiences and have always worked to build on the ones already acquired.

Furthermore, as a seasoned RE investor, I do various things in the RE business. As discussed in the previous chapters, I buy and sell RE investment properties. I fix distressed properties and turn around and flip and sometimes I may decide to put tenants in a particular property.

Coming back to my slightly more than 12 years experience in the RE business, I can always work into a property and be able to tell whether it is over-priced or priced within the market value. Most sellers over-price their properties when they are not desperate to sell.

Lender would only finance the appraised market value and will not finance anything more than the market value.

As an investor, it is my responsibility to keep up with the news and reading up on materials in order to keep up on what's going on in the business. I have to keep up with the changes in the market as it affects the RE business.

Inspecting properties are some of the things that I do as a RE investor. I can walk into a distressed property for inspection and take a walk through in and out of the property and be able to come up with roughly how much it might cost to do a fix-up in the house, without checking the plumbing systems if the water is not turned on and without checking the electricals when the power is not turned on.

My success as a RE investor depends on a variety of things: how I relate to people, how transparent I am when it comes to doing transactions, how honest and trustworthy I am when it comes to doing business with people. Keeping a good name and making sure my reputation is intact is very important to me as a businessman.

As a seasoned investor I am in business for myself. Regardless of how many hours I put in a week is something that I take extremely serious and try to be very productive. An important part of establishing myself as a seasoned investor is instilling in me the knowledge and education with the necessary tools to do the job.

Another part of seeing myself as a seasoned investor to do the job, in my search for RE investments, I will be looking for three basic categories of sellers: sellers that are flexible, sellers that may become flexible, and sellers that are inflexible. It is very essential for me to try and locate these sellers when I am doing my research to buy properties. I have always believed that establishing and advertising myself as a RE investor, flexible sellers will always come. Using business cards, flyers and newspaper ads for forms of advertisement is powerful. With business cards they can create a professional image and tell people the nature of your business. With flyers it allows the opportunity to include more things, and with the newspaper ad you are letting more people know you are in the RE business.

Banks are good sources of locating flexible sellers. They own a lot of properties as a result of foreclosures. Properties owned by banks are known as R.E.O.s (Real Estate Owned). I have dealt with a few banks on REOs. Banks are willing to negotiate because they would like to get rid of the properties at their disposal. Whenever I find myself going to the bank for the REOs, I do get prepared for some serious negotiations.

Furthermore, I have learned to work well with RE agents. They can go a long way in trying to help to find investment properties. The benefits of working with them are that they are: saving me time, using their resources to find properties at good locations.

As a seasoned investor, I have made it a point of duty to drive around town once in a while trying to locate some good neighborhoods that would be lucrative for investing. Sometimes when I am in some neighborhoods, I am taking notes of businesses, schools, etc. around the area. Also, I do stop to chat with people in the area.

Furthermore, as an investor who has been in the business more than 12 years, I have learned how to have a system in place that I use to pre-qualify a seller and his property for sale with making a telephone call. I do this to make sure a particular property fits my profile. If not I don't want to waste my time going to take a look at the property. When I contact a seller, I don't want to be wasting a lot of time. After exchanging greetings with him or her, I then go straight to the questions that require immediate answers. The questions that are being asked are phrased in a way not to be offensive. A good way of having a good conversation with the seller is to listen carefully. In the course of pre-qualifying the property I do come up with the following questions. I start by introducing myself and move on by asking some questions like:

- What is the size of the house?

- Does it have a garage?'

- How many bathrooms does it have?

- What is the asking price?

- Does it have a fence?

Most of the time, I don't get into the financing aspect of the property since most people are reluctant to give detailed financial information on their property. Once I have received the answers to the questions then I know that I have with me some information that would be helpful in making an informed decision.

In the final analysis, it's very imperative for me to analyze properties and determine which ones to buy and the ones to exit from, and which ones will be profitable ventures for me to pursue. I have established an exit strategy of backing out of a property that I am not interested in buying. Furthermore, in looking at a property to see if I may buy, I am thinking in my head whether to flip the property during renovation or complete the renovation and rent it out or sell. Sometimes it depends on what is going on at that particular time.

Also, as a seasoned investor, I have learned how to do a lease option in the RE business. Lease Option means when I have a property and lease it out to a tenant with the option of the tenant purchasing the property after one or two years, depending on what is stipulated in the contract. In most cases part of the rental payments may be going towards a down payment to purchase the property. Also, in some situations the fix-up may be going towards the down payment. It is very imperative for me to record the lease agreement with the county once it is written in order to avoid any unnecessary problems. It provides some form of peace between me and the potential buyer.

Carlton, in his book advises that the lease agreement should be typed or clearly printed in order to protect all the parties involved. He further stated that in a lease agreement there should be a <u>Right to Sublease</u>: "You should always make certain that your lease option will give you the right to sublease the property to another tenant." He also stated the <u>Right to Assign</u>: "Assignment is the right to transfer the contract and all of your rights to someone else. To avoid any misunderstanding or litigation, you should make sure that the right to assign the contract is spelled out in your lease option contract." Finally, he mentioned the <u>Right to Extend</u>: "Some lease . . . under which the option may be extended. This is known as an extension clause . . ." In the final analysis, some contracts may say that the extension of the lease option is prohibited and some may be silent on this point.

<u>Managing Properties</u>

As a seasoned RE investor one of the things I have done is to manage properties. I have managed people's properties in the past, but at a point it starts to become a headache that I had to give it up. Property Management is one of the most critical parts of RE investing. When one gets into property management, you will run into different kinds of tenants. Tenants will take advantage of you if you let them. To protect yourself and make the management process easier, you have to make certain that they understand where the line is drawn in a clearly defined lease. If they go beyond that point, they can expect a penalty.

From a management perspective, rental collections can be a nuisance and very frustrating. Tenants paying rent on time is always a problem. When the late fees are imposed, it is a problem also collecting on the late fees. When it comes to evicting tenants that is another long and complicated process. Now to God be the Glory that I have given up the idea of managing other people's properties, but focus on mine. Before a tenant moves into any of my properties, a lease agreement needs to be completed and I have the responsibility of explaining the lease agreement to make sure there is a clear understanding of what the lease agreement is all about. Once the lease agreement is signed by the parties involved, I have to make sure it is enforced whenever necessary.

Chapter 5

Having a Power Team

Working with a powerful team in the RE business is very advantageous. Working with the right people is very imperative to me. I do take my time in hiring a team that I would be comfortable working with. For me to be successful in the business, I have to work with people that I can trust and rely on to give me good and accurate information.

Putting a team together is always an on-going process. As the dynamics of the RE business changes then the team that I work with will continue to change. As an investor, I have learned how to utilize money and time to help assemble qualified people to help run my business in order to save time more effectively.

Finding a Reliable RE Agent

During the course of my RE business, I have worked with various RE agents. Having a good working relationship with them is very vital for me. When a property that I am interested in purchasing is listed with an agent, I may want to have my own agent working with me to represent my best interests on a particular deal. My relator has access to the

Multiple Listing Service (MLS) and can pull out listings for me at any time. This is a good source for locating great deals. My relator helps me pull up sold properties in the location of where I am trying to purchase a property, thereby giving me the opportunity to do comparables as to the property that I am interested in purchasing. This also gives me an idea of the market value of properties in an area.

The properties on the MLS does include pictures and information about the property, including the address of the property, the number of bedrooms and baths, square footage and other valuable amenities. Also, in the MLS there might be special terms the seller may consider.

Finding the Right Lawyer

Finding a trustworthy and reliable lawyer is equally important to me. Not just finding any lawyer. The lawyer I am finding must be knowledgeable in the RE business. He has to be someone who is familiar with RE contracts. A lawyer who understands how to do a thorough title search and be able to close on a deal is very important.

In finding the right lawyer, I need one who would be able to vigorously represent me if a law suit is brought against me or if am suing someone.

The Right Banker

Finding the right banker to assist in the RE business is very vital. I do take time to talk with various bankers to be able to determine who may be in a position to work with me. Building a good working relationship with a banker is very important to me.

The Right Contractor/ Handyman

Finding the right contractor or the right handyman to work with is very important to me. When it comes to fixing up my properties, I have always used a handyman. Most of them can equally do what a contractor can do. It is very important to me that a handyman that I use would be someone I can really trust. I usually locate handymen from fellow investors. My handyman gives me a detailed report on the fix-ups that are needed on a particular property.

If there is any evidence of the roof leaking, foundation problems or roof that looks unstable, I will bring in a contractor to definitely take a look at it and provide me with a detailed report. Sometimes I may bring in a building inspector on board to help with updating various building codes.

Working with Other Investors

I have always enjoyed working with the other RE investors. I see them as partners, mentors and business associates. Having a cordial relationship with other investors has helped me to determine the best areas in which to invest, and the areas to avoid. I have always enjoyed exchanging ideas with them. I have always made it a point of duty to locate other investors that I can always work with.

The Right Appraiser

Finding the right appraiser is very important in the RE business. I use appraisers to be able to appraise a property and provide me with the market value of a particular property. I always look for an appraiser who can give an honest market value of a property.

The Right Surveyors

Anytime I am using a financial institution to get some money for my RE business, a survey would be required. The surveyor's responsibility is basically to determine the boundaries of a property. The boundaries are then marked with stakes. Surveyors can provide valuable information about local properties.

Finally, as far as building up a team in the RE business, I am always looking for good people to work with. Whenever I go to business seminars or business related events, I am always handing out business cards, trying to establish new contacts every day. In the final analysis, having a good powerful team leads to a successful business.

CHAPTER 6

How the Financial Crisis of 2008 Affected the Real Estate Business

The impact of the 2008 financial crisis on the RE business was very devastating and was felt across the country. When the financial downturn began, cities like Las Vegas, Miami, and many big states were hit first before other small states started feeling the impact. The downturn has led to some layoffs in the RE business, which have in turn lead to a decrease in the purchase of RE properties. As a result of this downturn, consumer spending slowed down and the demand to even go take a look at a property before purchasing also slowed down. Furthermore, with the crisis, potential buyers are in a good position to negotiate better. Buyers with strong credit history are able to negotiate better than they were a couple of years ago.

The financial crisis of 2008 forced many companies to go bankrupt. Many people were losing their properties, making those properties available and vacant for a long time.

The availability of many properties made the prices to

go down. Many went down below market value. I had a bad experience with some of my properties. After the fixup of some of my investment properties, the market value, instead of going up, remained stagnant or even went down. In most cases, when I compared the properties in the neighborhood to my properties, I realized that they were not comparable to the ones in the area. The market value of the ones sold a few years back, had a market value that was reasonable.

I did not realize that the financial crisis has seriously affected the real estate market until I had a horrible experience. The experience was that there was a distressed property that I purchased for about forty thousand dollars in a fairly good neighborhood. I spent about ten to eleven thousand dollars to fix it in order to bring up the value. The comparables in this area were in the high eighty to low ninety thousands. I listed the property for seventy nine thousand dollars so that I could sell it easily. Potential buyers were pricing the property for high forties to low fifties. At this time, I really realized that the RE market was extremely bad. This incident was happening in the middle of 2009. When I added the price of purchasing the property, and the price of fix-up compared to the price people were willing to pay, one can say that it does not make any sense. I am in the RE business to make money and not to lose money.

The financial crisis of 2008 also known as the global financial crisis is considered by many economists to be the worst financial crisis since the Great Depression of the 1920s. (Allison, p. 41) This resulted in the threat of total collapse of large financial institutions, the bailouts of banks by national government, . . . around the world. For many areas, the RE market suffered, resulting in evictions, foreclosures, and prolonged unemployment. The crisis played a significant role in the franchise of key businesses, declines in consumer wealth estimated in trillions of US dollars ... in economic activity leading to the 2008 Global Recession. (Allison, p. 43)

The bursting of the United States housing bubble, which peaked in 2006, caused the values of securities tied to US real estate pricing to plummet, changing financial institutions globally. (Milton, p. 18). The financial crisis was triggered by a complex interplay of government policies that encouraged home ownerships. This was providing easier access to loans for subprime borrowers. (Milton, p. 70)

Financial innovations enabled institutions and investors around the world to invest in the US housing market. As the housing prices declined, major global financial institutions that borrowed and invested heavily in subprime reported significant losses. (Milton, p.7) Falling prices also resulted in homes worth less than the mortgage loan, providing a financial incentive to enter foreclosure. The on-going foreclosure epidemic that began in the late 2007 in the US continues to drain wealth from consumers and erodes the financial strength of banking institutions. Defaults and losses on other loan types also increased significantly as the crisis expanded from the housing markets to other parts of the economy. (Milton, p. 82)

By September of 2008, the average US housing prices had declined by over 20% from the mid 2006 peak. As prices declined, borrowers with adjustable rate mortgages could not refinance to avoid the higher payments associated with rising interest rates. During this financial crisis, lenders began foreclosure proceedings on nearly 1.3 million properties. By the end of 2008, about 9.2% of all US mortgages outstanding were either delinquent or in foreclosure. By the end of 2009, this had risen to 14.4%. (Blindes, p. 30)

In the years leading to the financial crisis, home owners were able to extract significant equity in their homes. Once the financial downturn happened and the collapse of real estate/housing prices, they were not able to get any equity from their properties.

The financial crisis has been so devastating that a home owner who does not have any equity may find him or herself in a serious default risk. In the case of business, their creditworthiness depends on their future profits. Profit prospects looked much worse towards the end of 2008 than they did towards the end of 2007. Many financial institutions were at the brink of collapse. Consumers, businesses, and property owners were having a hard time getting the credit they needed.

The 2008 financial crisis further caused the housing prices to continue to fall. They fell drastically especially in the areas in which they had risen. Rising interest rates led to rising mortgage payments. As the interest rates were going up, the market values of properties were going down. Mortgages continued to go up and when property owners could no longer afford to make their payments, it was possible for lenders to go in and repossess the property which eventually would be foreclosed.

Thomas Sowell in his book, <u>The Housing Boom and Burst:</u> stated that large-scale foreclosures meant falling home prices as the foreclosed homes added to the supply without any corresponding increase in demand. He stated that the "fully half of all existing homes sold in the USA in December 2008 were foreclosures unloaded by banks at fire-sale prices." A serious decline in the real estate and housing prices continued into 2009. (Home Price Market for October 2008, p. 9) compared to October of the previous year, declined more sharply than at any time in the two decades' history of that index. In the index of 2008, many metropolitan cities showed housing prices declined by more than 25 per cent compared to October of the previous year. (Home Price Index for October, 2008, p. 11)

Finally, the financial crisis has not only been devastating for the real estate and housing markets, but has affected the entire economy. The construction of new homes plunged. Furniture dealers folded, and hardware stores were suffering. Unemployment rates kept going up as people continued to lose their jobs. Even young graduates after graduating from college did not find jobs, a situation which might lead to thinking about engaging in dubious activities.

When the RE and housing market got really bad, I got into mediations and Human Resources Management (HRM). I still do RE investments, but have scaled down a little bit. It is a business one cannot go wrong. <u>To God be the Glory that things are turning back around</u>. Unemployment is going down; the economy is getting better; interest rates are low; and non-investors are getting back to RE investments.

CHAPTER 7

Financing Real Estate Deals

One of the things someone should keep in mind while getting into RE investments is how to finance the deals. What can make or break a prospective Real Estate Investor is funds and where to find the funds to do the deals.

There are conventional and non-conventional ways to finance a RE transaction. Some of the conventional ways of financing a RE deal include going through the banks, mortgage lenders, insurance companies, and pension funds. While some of the non-conventional ways to finance a deal may include private lenders, hard money lenders, or corporate lenders, etc.

To locate private lenders, one can always ask around. They are the wealthy folks who want to put their excess cash to work for them earning better than bank rates. Some private lenders may receive up to 18% on their loan. According to Hicks, you can also use a finder to locate private lenders. A finder is a firm who finds things for other people. Thus, you can ask a finder to locate money that you can borrow and invest in RE. You don't have to pay the finder's fee until after you obtain the money you need. (Hicks, p. 38)

Also in his book, Hicks indicated that to make conventional mortgage money work, you have to:

- Negotiate to get the lowest interest rate;

- Avoid paying points. (1% of mortgage per point;

- Be a complete business person at all times;

- Fight against take outs . . . in which a lender gets part of the profits, (usually 1% or 2% for the life of the project).
(Hicks, p.16)

Based on my experience with conventional funding, when I submit a proposal for the funds to do a deal, I have to make sure that the documents are well typed and looking clean. I try as much as possible to be calm and cool when talking to a lender. I always make sure that the applications and loans are fully completed. Having a clear understanding of how the conventional funding works is very important when doing a RE deal.

Hicks identified "Home Equity", "Credit Card Loan", and using the internet to fund RE deals. Today lenders are excited over the "home equity," line of credit as well as the borrowers who are taking the loans. "Why don't you go with the money flow and get a home equity loan for your real estate . . . ." If you don't have a home, how can you get a home equity line of credit? Just try these Methods:

- Borrow using a relative's home as equity;

- Borrow using a partner's home;

- Offer a fee to a person who will borrow his or her home equity and loan to you;

- Run a classified ad in a local paper to find homeowners who might help.
  (Hicks, p. 45)

The whole idea of getting an equity loan is to have a home that can be used as a collateral.

Credit card is another way to get funds to be able to finance a RE deal. If you have a major credit card, you probably also have a line of credit on the card. You can use part of the funds from your credit card to finance your RE deal. As a credit card holder, remember that you can always use the money for whatever you want to do. Also, the interest on your credit card lines of the real estate business is tax deductible.

Internet is another source of locating funds to finance a RE deal. From the internet, one can be able to find additional lenders to assist in financing the RE business. If you don't have a personal computer, you can always go to the public library or a business center to search the websites. Many websites offer residential loans and some others offer loans for commercial real estate deals.

Working With A Mortgage Broker

Sometimes it takes time to get a good mortgage broker (MB), one can work with as far as financing the RE deals. It is very essential to work with a MB who has great experience working with investors and one who has access to different financing programs. Some MBs may have access to private funds that may not require being pre-qualified.

When one starts working with a MB on a deal, the broker may ask the prospective investor: Have you been pre-qualified or pre-approved? James Banks in his book summarized the two terms as follows: With pre-qualified, the MB is looking at your income and debt to see how much you can afford to pay the mortgage payment. Based on the information obtained, the MB can tell you the maximum amount you can get. The MB will follow with a pre-qualification letter stating the amount of loan you will be receiving; however, the loan is not guaranteed until some other documents have been checked out. (Banks, p. 62)

Pre-approval is considered a step towards getting the financing. Income, credit and employment information will be checked out. Other considerations such as title work, approval etc. will be factored in before the loan is granted. Once everything checks out, an approval letter would be given to the borrower to be taken to the lender or bank. (Banks, p. 63)

Working with a good and a reliable MB would make your RE financing go very smoothly.

Chapter 8

Doing Real Estate in a Foreign Country Especially Nigeria

In this chapter, I will discuss what it takes to do a real estate deal in a foreign country such as Nigeria. I am choosing Nigeria because I am originally from Nigeria and have done a few real estate deals there myself.

For anyone to start thinking about conducting any form of business in a foreign land or deciding to enter in the RE business in another country such as Nigeria, the person needs to have a clear understanding of the rules, laws, policies, and different kinds of regulations to make sure what he or she wants to get into.

Once you start getting involved with RE investments in Nigeria, it's imperative to be on the alert and be quite aware of your surroundings. Today RE business is very lucrative in Nigeria because the country is presently faced with increasing population. As a result, shelter and accommodations will be provided for this increasing population. Lands and properties would continue to appreciate.

Real estate investments are always good for someone

who is looking forward to a good deal. That means, that if you have the funds to invest and ready to have some patience, you may do well in the RE investments. Most of the time RE transactions in Nigeria requires huge amount of money. Due to the huge amount of money involved in the RE business, some people may decide to team up with people who have the same kind of dreams and experiences with them. Real estate business is good and very lucrative in Nigeria as well as in many other countries. If a business is run well, the person will be spinning in money. If one decides to go in the business in a country like Nigeria, the person is getting in the right direction towards becoming a world class business man.

Based on the RE investments that I have experienced in Nigeria, I will surely say that the experiences have been awesome. For me to do RE investments in Nigeria was not a decision that was taken lightly. I have always had passion for RE business and have always liked buying distressed properties (ugly buildings), because that is where the money is.

As I write this book, people are buying lands and properties and leaving them for sometime for them to appreciate so that they can be sold much later with some serious profits.

There have been people who have profited immensely from buying lands, buying an old or dilapidated or a new structure, or a structure that may need serious renovations or even structures that are under construction. Sometimes one can invest in a new structure that may need serious renovations or even structures that are under construction.

It works out well as long as you have at the back of your mind what you would like to do with a particular property or structure.

Location is very imperative when you do RE business in Nigeria. You would like to consider a prime location or an area that would be developed within a short period of time. As an investor, I am quite aware of the fact that a prime location is very important when it comes to RE investing. Anywhere, including the United States, location is very important.

The success of RE business is guaranteed in Nigeria if done well at the proper location. Advertising your RE business is equally important.

Although RE investments in Nigeria may be lucrative, if you don't have substantial amount of money that's ok. However, you need some funds to get started and to be able to start well and start moving in the right direction. If you don't have enough funds to get started, you can always join a RE investment club, get a loan from the bank, a friend or from a family member. Once the funds are in place and a good deal is embarked on, the rest is history.

Setbacks

Despite real estate business being lucrative in Nigeria, there are still some setbacks and pitfalls. Some of the setbacks are as follows: sometimes there are many regulations, decrees and laws affecting the value of properties in Nigeria. The growing population in the country has been unbelievable. This boils down to the problem of finding properties for them.

Immediate availability of funds may be a setback when there is an immediate and a good deal to take care of.

Getting certificate of occupancy (CFO) may sometimes be very bureaucratic and take a long process which in most cases, may require the Governor's consent.

Furthermore, it is important to be aware of the fact that sometimes sellers who claim to own properties come up with fraudulent papers. This is why a thorough research is required before you buy any property in Nigeria.

In the final analysis, real estate investments still remain a business one can get into and still make a reasonable amount of money. The only thing is that at some point, you need to have some patience, especially when you want to sell. You cannot go wrong when it comes to RE investments. I am saying this from experience.

Chapter 9

Faith in God and the Power of Prayer

In this last chapter of this book, I intend to discuss my faith in God and the power of prayer. I will also enclose some biblical quotes. My focus will be more on the biblical side.

The American Heritage College dictionary defines faith in various ways: 1) "Confident belief in the truth, value, or trustworthiness of a person, an idea, or a thing." 2) "Belief that does not rest on logical proof or material evidence." 3) "Loyalty to a person or thing." 4) "The theological virtue defined as secure belief in God and a trusting acceptance of God's will." My main focus will be on the fourth definition.

Reverend Paul Tillich, in his book <u>Dynamics Of Faith</u>: stated that "faith is the state of ultimately concerned: the dynamics of faith are the dynamics of man's ultimate concern. Man like every living being is concerned about many things, above all those which condition his very existence, such as food and shelter." However, man in contrast to other living beings has spiritual concerns. (Tillich, p. 2).

Furthermore, Reverend Kenneth E. Hagin, in his book:

Walking In Faith: talks about faith in the sense that "if you believe in God's word, you will act as if it is true." (Hagin, p. 4). "Now faith is the substance of things hoped for, the evidence of things not seen." (Hebrews 11:1). Hagin further indicated that "faith makes the difference between defeat and victory in a Christian's life." The Holy Bible in the New and Old testaments shows us how God's people accomplished many things just by putting their faith in action.

The book of Joshua, in the Old Testament, shows us how faith works in action:

The Lord said to Joshua: "I have given Jericho into your hand, ... You shall march around the city all you men of war; you shall go all around the city once. This you shall do six days. Seven priests shall bear seven trumpets . . . and the seventh day, you shall march around the city seven times and the priests shall blow the trumpets . . . . It shall come to pass, when they make a long blast . . . . and when you hear the sound of the trumpets . . ., then the wall of the city will fall down flat." (Joshua 6:2-5).

Reverend Hagin, in his book, analyzed that given the city of Jericho "into thine hand" does not mean that Joshua and the Children of Israel could sit back and relax and not do anything for the city to become theirs. He further stated that instructions were given to them by God on how to go about possessing the land. They had to believe in the word "faith" and act on it. Hagin summarizes "faith in action" by stating that for something to happen spiritually and to come to pass, we have to "pray, believe, and act; then something will happen."

The gospel according to Luke in the New Testament,

talks about "faith in action."

"Then behold, men brought on a bed a man who was paralyzed . . . And when they could not find how they might bring him in because of the crowd, they went up on the house top and let him down with his bed through . . . before Jesus. When he saw their faith, He said to him, "man your sins are forgiven." (Luke 5:18-20) "But . . . the Son of man has power on earth to forgive sins). He said to the man who was paralyzed, "I say to you arise, take up your bed and go to your house."

Immediately, he rose up before them, took up what he had been lying on and departed to his own house, glorifying God." (Luke 5:24-25).

Hagin summarized this by indicating that the sick man demonstrated great faith. "When Jesus told him to rise, he began to move and when he did, healing was the result." If he had refused to act on the word, he may not have received healing. Because the acted, he received healing.

As a Christian and having lived in the United States for more than twenty years, I have gone through tribulations, ups and downs, all kinds of changes, people encouraging or discouraging me from doing one thing or the other, trying to put me down for no just cause no matter the situation. I have always had faith in God. God has given me one hundred percent strength in all my endeavors. I have always sought God's favor and protection in all that I do. Having faith in God has kept me moving and moving in the right direction. Writing this book has not been by might nor by my own power, but "to God be the Glory."

CHAPTER 9

Faith in God and the Power of Prayer

In this last chapter of this book, I intend to discuss my faith in God and the power of prayer. I will also enclose some biblical quotes. My focus will be more on the biblical side.

The American Heritage College dictionary defines faith in various ways: 1) "Confident belief in the truth, value, or trustworthiness of a person, an idea, or a thing." 2) "Belief that does not rest on logical proof or material evidence." 3) "Loyalty to a person or thing." 4) "The theological virtue defined as secure belief in God and a trusting acceptance of God's will." My main focus will be on the fourth definition.

Reverend Paul Tillich, in his book <u>Dynamics Of Faith:</u> stated that "faith is the state of ultimately concerned: the dynamics of faith are the dynamics of man's ultimate concern. Man like every living being is concerned about many things, above all those which condition his very existence, such as food and shelter." However, man in contrast to other living beings has spiritual concerns. (Tillich, p. 2).

Furthermore, Reverend Kenneth E. Hagin, in his book:

properties for them.

Immediate availability of funds may be a setback when there is an immediate and a good deal to take care of.

Getting certificate of occupance (CFO) may sometimes be very bureaucratic and take a long process which in most cases, may require the Governor's consent.

Furthermore, it is important to be aware of the fact that sometimes sellers who claim to own properties come up with fraudulent papers. This is why a thorough research is required before you buy any property in Nigeria.

In the final analysis, real estate investments still remain a business one can get into and still make a reasonable amount of money. The only thing is that at some point, you need to have some patience, especially when you want to sell. You cannot go wrong when it comes to RE investments. I am saying this from experience.

By God's grace, I have always let go the past and live each day by faith. I always expect God's Devine favor and miracle. By faith I have always tried to keep a good attitude even when things are going the wrong way. I have learned that no matter who is trying to push me down, I need to stay up.

I believe that a negative spirit dries up someone's happiness and weaken the immune system. By faith, I have learned to keep a positive attitude no matter the situation. Keeping faith alive is very important to me. Faith has sustained me and my family, including my career. I thank "God for being a faithful God."

Biblical Quotes on Faith

1. Now faith is the substance of things hope for, the evidence of things not seen. (Hebrews 11:1).

2. So then faith comes by hearing and hearing by the word of God. (Romans 10:17).

3. Therefore, leaving the discussion . . . . of Christ, let us go on to perfection . . . foundation of repentance from dead works of faith toward God. (Hebrews 6:1).

4. But without faith it is impossible to please God, for he who comes to God must believe that he is a rewarder of those who seek him. (Hebrews 11:6).

Power of Prayer

The power of prayer is awesome in any situation. Whenever I am praying a powerful prayer, I can always feel it and know it helped put my enemies in a state of confusion and anarchy. Through prayers, God has been able to reveal many things to me. Praying these days and even praising his name is very vital to me and it is giving God all the glory. Furthermore, when I am praying, I believe that the devil is in trouble and God is releasing the power of Holy Ghost fire on demonic attacks.

Prayer could also be seen as being wide and deep. It is a communication with God. It occurs when one offers his heart's desire unto God in the name of our Lord Jesus Christ by the help of the Holy Spirit. (Psalm 65:2).

Prayer could also be seen as a form of offering to God. This is so, especially the prayer of worship, praise and thanksgiving. People should not be too caught up in their personal affairs to the extent of forgetting to give quality time to God Almighty. Our physical and spiritual needs could be met by being obedient to his word. With prayer, we can receive things from God. (Jeremiah 33:3).

Dr. Myles Munroe, in his book: <u>Understanding The Purpose And Power of Prayer</u>: describes prayer as "the first global product of religion . . . ." "No matter how diverse the religions of the world may be, one common ritual and practice they all embrace is prayer." Munroe further indicates that to understand the principle of prayer, "it is necessary to understand the mind and the purpose of the Creator himself."

What Prayer is all About

- Prayer is man giving God the legal right to interfere in earth's affairs.

- Prayer is man giving heaven earthly license to influence earth.

- Prayer is man exercising his legal authority on Earth to invoke heaven's influence on the planet.
  (Munroe, 2002).

Prayer is the key to many things in life. It is the key to many hopeless situations in life. Once we understand our roles as God's people for the world and have dealt with areas in our lives that block prayer, we need to make sure we truly understand the power behind prayer.

Prayer is very necessary and it is an invitation to talk to God. It is an important part of God's purpose and it is something everybody should be able to go for.

Biblical Quotes on Prayer

1. And whatever you ask in my name, that I will do, that the Father may be glorified in the Son. If you ask anything in my name, I will do it.
   (John 14:13-14).

2. Peter was therefore kept in prison, but constant prayers were offered to God for him by the church.
   (Act 12:5).

3. If my people who are called . . . and pray and seek my face, and turn from their wicked ways . . . and will forgive their sin and will heal their land. (2 Chronicles 7:14).

4. Pray without ceasing, in everything give thanks, for this is the will of God in Christ Jesus for you. (I Thessalonians 5:17-18).

   Therefore, I say to you whatever things you ask when you pray, believe that you receive them and you will have them. Whenever you stand praying, if you have anything against anyone, forgive him . . . . (Mark 11:24-26).

Conclusion

With a humble spirit, I bring this book to its conclusion. It has not been easy writing, but "To God be the Glory." With hectic business and family schedules, the time spent writing this book has been quite challenging. Reflecting on my experiences as a Real Estate investor has been awesome.

Once again, I want to thank family members, friends, colleagues, and my church members, who have continuously encouraged me while writing this book. May we all continue to remain blessed in JESUS' Name!!!

REFERENCES

Allison, John A. (2013) The Financial Crisis and The Free Market Cure.
Mcgraw Hill Publishing Company.

Banks, James. (2004) Guide to RE Investing.
Crown Publishing, New York.

Blinder, Allen S. (2013) The Financial Crisis,
The response and the work ahead.
The Penguin Press.

Effros, Bill. (2007) What it takes to sell your home in 5 days.
Workman Publishing—New York.

Hicks, Tyler G. (2005) How to make millions in RE in three years. Peniguin Press.

Milton, Stephene. (2010) Crisis in the Real Estate Market
Published by Peniguin Group.

Sheets, Carleton.(2000) How to buy your first home.
Author-House.

Sowell, Thomas. (2009) The housing boom and bust.
Basic book Publishing: A member of the Rerseus Group.

INDEX

A

Adjustable Rate 39
Appraiser 35
Auction 11, 12

B

Banks, James 10, 11, 45,
Brokers 2, 12
Buyer 2, 3

C

Certificate of Occupancy . 49
Comparables 38
Contractor 2, 35
Credit Card 44
Credit Card Loan 43

D

Deductible 44

E

Effros 21

F

Fence 30
Financial Crisis 37, 38
Financial Innovations 39
Fix-Ups 8, 9, 14, 19, 28, 38
Flipping 19
Foreclosure 41
For Sale by Owner
 (FSBO) 20

G

Global Financial 38
Global Recession 39
Governor 49

H

Handyman 15, 35

L

Lawyer 2, 34
Lease Agreement 31
Lease Option .. 19, 20, 25, 31
Location 3, 8, 48

M

Market Value 2, 37, 40
Maslow, Abraham 4, 5
Mediations 41
Medical Expenses 11
Mortgagee 10, 39
Mortgagor 10
Mortgage Broker 44
Munroe, Myles 54
Multiple Listings 20

P

Power Team 33
Pre-qualification 24

R

Real Estate Agent ... 8, 20, 29
Real Estate Business .. 1, 2, 3, 5, 29, 35
Real Estate Investment .. 1, 2, 13 48
Real Estate Market 38
Real Estate Transaction 47
Renovation 12
Rental Collections 32
Real Estate Owned (REO) 29

S

Sales Contract 14
Seasoned Investor 27, 28
Seller 14, 22

U

Ubaezonu, Eugene v
Ubaezonu, Janet v

V

Vandalizing 12

About the Author

Dr. Somto Ubezonu hails from a town called Nnewi in Anambra State, Nigeria. He is the second son of six children born to the Honorable Justice Eugene C. and Mrs. Janet N. Ubaezonu. Dr. Ubezonu received his Elementary and High School Education in Nigeria, after which he proceeded to a private College in Oxford, England to complete his A-levels. From there, he proceeded to the United States where he attended various universities. He holds a Bachelor of Arts Degree in Political Science, MPA and a Ph.D., in Public Administration. He also holds certifications in Human Resources Management as well as in Mediations.

Dr. Ubezonu has worked with various employers in different capacities since residing in the United States. He is currently the Chief Executive Officer and Principal Partner of CU Consulting Services in Durham, North Carolina. He has had an opportunity to lecture in the Cape Program at Shaw University, Raleigh, NC.

Having faith in God has enabled Dr. Somto Ubezonu to accomplish great things in life. He attributes these accomplishments to God and to the support and encouragement given to him by his parents and family members. He is a very committed and dedicated individual who takes it upon himself as a challenge to work seriously on any given project or assignment. He has worked on projects within and outside the United States.

Dr. Ubezonu has gone through challenges, ups and downs, tribulations and obstacles to be where he is today. He tries as much as possible to stay out of trouble by keeping himself busy with more important things in life.

Finally, Dr. Ubezonu is a person who respects others, regardless of their age, race, ethnic, educational background, income, or status in life. As far as he is concerned, everyone remains equal in God's eyes.

www.ingramcontent.com/pod-product-compliance
Lightning Source LLC
Chambersburg PA
CBHW031535210526
45464CB00003B/1014